A Place for Nicholas

Written by Lucy Floyd
Illustrated by David McPhail

HARCOURT BRACE & COMPANY

Orlando Atlanta Austin Boston San Francisco Chicago Dallas New York
Toronto London

Nicholas wanted a place.
Not just any place.
He wanted his own place.

"You have this house," Dad said.
"But everybody is here," Nicholas said.

"You have this yard," Kelly said.
"But everybody is here," Nicholas said.

"You have this room," Mom said.
"But Jeff is here," Nicholas said.

"I'll make a place for you," Jeff said.
"You? You are too little," Nicholas said.

"Come back soon. You'll see," Jeff said.

Nicholas did see.
And now he has his very own place.